The State of Things

Alice Pembroke

BookLeaf
Publishing
India | USA | UK

Presentation by *BookLeaf Publishing*

Web: www.bookleafpub.com

E-mail: info@bookleafpub.com

ISBN: 978-93-5744-352-4

First edition 2022

ACKNOWLEDGEMENT

Thank you to my friends and family for the never-ending support, without you I would not be here.

the Meaning of it All

open your eyes

to the quiet moment of realisation
a whisper of what truly is

the meaning of it all
staring back at you so simply

but you will fan away the smoky picture
i know you will
acceptance is out of the question
for it is unknown
and you are built on fear

but one day, when you wake up in a new world
hinted so subtly at you in this one
tell everyone that i said hi
and that i tried to open your ignorant eyes
but, like everyone,
you could only accept the meaning of true living
once you had died

blockbuster

i know you'd given up
on that random Tuesday night
and i bet you thought 'this is it'
the final end to your year-long fight

how anticlimactic
would it be
for a person like you, so full of life
to pass in your sleep

you will die not today and not tomorrow
and not any day soon
i know it

and i will watch movies with you for hours on
end
and you will laugh-cry again
and one day you will find someone who treats
you right
who you won't text me about at midnight
to fearfully complain of their wrongs
but to say 'i've made it, i've made it, i've made it'
and look at how far you've come

and i can see the life you're going to have

a movie in my head
and it's the best i've ever seen
one of those fantasy worlds
that make you want to jump through the screen

but it is real
and fuck, it's awesome
you've got to see it
you've got to stick around and live it

and i know it's hard,
those vile words everyone tells you
but i say them from inside of my soul

but even more so
i say, i plead, i beg
you must stick around to watch the credits roll

the memory of birth

like any other child
i don’t recall the moment i was born
and what it felt like to come into this world

but i do recall being
maybe six
and having no one to play my favourite game
with
and there i was
a screaming newborn in a world of confusion
who knows nothing but this aching feeling
inside

and turning ten
and told by friends i wasn’t fun anymore
and suddenly, i had a room full of strangers
staring at me;
everyone foreign, even those people i once knew
and i thought that to be fair; because i would
stare at a crying baby, too

and i know that every child
faces this pain like me
but these moments would define and birth
the person i came to be

i’ve seen pictures
and felt a warmth inside
from the post-birth happiness
but it feels like a lie

held and loved and nurtured
every possible moment i could’ve been
but i'm still haunted by the nightmare
of my very first memory

voodoo doll

kiss your stuffed animals goodnight
and place your dolls upright

because somewhere out there
is a boy with a butter knife who will rip out the stuffing
and carve out the heart

and his sickeningly sweet mother will stitch it up
then kiss his cheek with a laugh

and she'll be amused
and he'll be excused

and it won't matter because it's a doll
and without a mouth
it can't tell anyone about what he had done
so at the end of the day
as always,
the little boy had won

dear God

observe one another's cries for help
then cry "help" to a god not Godly enough to
listen

but just Godly enough to deserve worship
and credit for our good days

you are to blame for the bad ones
i will taint your good name
i will spit on it
i will scream it in vain
watch me

i am sorry
i beg for Your Forgiveness
In the name of the Father
hear my reconciliation

O my god I am truly sorry
For I have sinned
And with the help of Your Grace,

i will sin again
and again and again

so condemn me, my Lord
send me to hell
i have lived there from the beginning

Amen.

missed dose

someone is trying to tell me something
the who or what i am still unsure

but there is a hint
in the time that my watch displays
when I feel the need to check it

another clue in the rumblings of the television
if you re-jumble the news reporter's words
to form cryptic sentences
that will make sense soon enough

mind-maps cover my walls
as i try to keep track of it all:
the time between each flicker of a broken
streetlight,
the name of each song that plays when i enter a
store,
pictures of number plates that drive past me
extra slowly,
i'm careful not to miss a single clue that they
show me

and after endless study
i found what was being communicated to me
all along
it all makes sense now
every little sign pointed to one short instruction:

"take your medication."

sink or swim

it was an effortless
thoughtless decision
as i threw the pebble

and i had heard about the downfall
of an ex-friend of a friend
who did the same
and breaking news stories
about the consequential tidal waves

but that won't happened to me
and i know
'that's what they all say'
but it really won't
this isn't some freak case

so i watched it skim across the water
happy little dips
until the ripples got larger
and then it started to sink

shrugging, i left the crime scene
thinking the damage was done
but as i felt my throat close up
i realised it'd only just begun

water filling my body
as i drowned from the inside
but i knew it would ease the pain
if i became one with the raging tide

so i lived underwater
month after month
watching life through glassy ocean eyes
and lying to the ones i loved

and on another endless day
after i'd lost track of time
i spotted an island offshore
and the decision was mine

sink
or swim

and although fluid still filled my lungs
and it would be far easier to plunge
back into the cold home i'd known for months

i decided slowly drowning wasn't
how i wanted to live anymore
so i picked myself up
and began my journey to the shore.

there is no "i"

an empty canvas
a wordless novel

unknowingly,
the people around me
pick paintbrush or pen
and help bring me to life

telling a story
in which every movement is scripted
for its desired audience

i've become a forgotten side character
half-dead, half-alive
constantly waiting for their designated screen time

but when the book is put down
and there is no one to show off to anymore
and all i am left with is a broken mind
that fails at making something of its own

i realise i never learnt how to paint or write
just how to act and lie
and in these lonely moments there is nothing to
me
quietly, there is no "i"

that funny feeling

that funny feeling
when the days start to merge
and you get that uncontrollable urge

and you wonder
when did it go from something you talked about
while making jokes
to the very thing you'll name check
in your goodbye note?

somewhere in the whirlwind of days passed
and people leaving your needs until last
while the sun went down on another day you
didn't realise you were living

it dawned on you
that it was all a bit too real
and that this may truly be the only thing
you will ever feel

and suddenly
that funny feeling
wasn't so funny anymore

it became more of a deafening silence
that resembled the end
of it all.

The Road Travelled

two roads diverged in a yellow wood,
and involuntary, i travelled the one no one did,
the one no one should

navigated the bush thick with thorns and vines
tangling and trapping my body
with every pathetic step i took

i crawled,
begging for the road more travelled
begging for some guidance and relief
for some company
for someone like me

and then i found it
through a golden lit escape route
hiding between the unkempt bushes

so with bruises and cuts and a body i didn't
recognise
i hobbled along with my peers, mimicking their
stride
making conversation about the weather
but with no acknowledgement and no relief from
inside

studying their posture and the beat of their feet
on the smooth gravel,
i continued playing along
as if i was like them
as if this is the path i, too, was born to travel

with no memory of where i came from,
but the vague feeling that it wasn't here;
my bones broke and i fell down
and collapsing on the side of the pretty neat road
the lights went out.

and i don't know when this happened
but i have never felt the same again
i wish i came from the same place as everyone
else
i wish i could be like my friends

time machine

take me back to the very moment everything
changed
please, i beg of you
tell me it's all a big bad dream
and if it's not
invent me a time machine
and let me go back

even if i cannot change the course
let me sit
for just five short minutes and mourn
what is in front of me
and the person i could've been

let me look myself in the eyes
i won't tell her everything is going to be okay
because this is not for her sake
it is for mine

i'll say i'm sorry kid,
but everything is not going to be fine

i won't hug her
that's for another day
i will walk around my house
interact with life the way it should have stayed
and then sob in my childhood bed and watch it
change

i'll soak it up, i swear
i'll never need to go back
i just want to feel for a moment
the very things i've been chasing
the very things that i lack

if nothing else, i'll slap the kid across the face
say you better enjoy this, and chant
remember it remember it remember it
because i fucking can't

r/a

you can tell me you won't leave
and i'll pretend to believe you

but they're talking again
our ghosts
yours is saying what you won't

what i know you want to tell me
what i wake up every day and wait to hear

because the only truth i'll believe
is what my ghost whispers in my ear

remember me neatly

my clothes covered the floor
from the wall to the door
no room to walk

and in the state i was in
it never even bothered me
i would leave my room in this mess
for days
for weeks
or until time felt like it didn't exist

but one day
after a month
i decided to clean it
there was a newfound drive in me
that made my family so happy

but sadly
as they would soon realise
it wasn't so i could live with a clean room
it was so
i would die with one

pretty lies

the excitement of a new room
the genuine pledge to change
empty promises
so that i'll stay

i wish i didn't eat up your pretty lies
i know that they'll turn bad in a few days
and i'll be sick to my stomach for weeks
but each time it feels different
so i divulge in them excitedly

as the years have gone by
you have ruined my body
my throat sore from the bile
teeth turned yellow when i smile

they ask me why i'm so cold to you now
but i have to keep my mouth closed
to keep myself alive
because i think that i will break
if i let you feed me one more pretty lie

the obligatory holiday poem

the scent of Aerogard tickles my nostrils
and the salt covers my wet hair
the soft sheets after a long day at the beach
with a stomach full from the barbecue
of burgers and sausages drenched in tomato
sauce
that satisfies something deep but simple within
the soul

waking up with that well rested taste in my
mouth
and the sun warming my bare legs
going on short walks to the cafe
and long swims covered in sunscreen
submerging in the warm water as it fulfils its
promise
to carry my bodyweight and stress

i forget this is how i was meant to live

instead of sweaty city buildings
the smell of sewers and cigarettes
and the fog from lazy cynical content
poisoning my creative mind

here i can breathe and think
i look up at the curing sunny sky
and while i know i can’t forever escape the city
i can sure as hell try

the apocalypse

i have this gut feeling that something
is very very wrong
i checked the news to see
if i was right
sure, disaster did strike
but this feeling warrants
something greater

now i'm sitting in my bedroom
and the walls are closing in
the end of the world is coming
i can feel it within

shitty love poem

i put on all these different faces
but looking at you with each one
is like falling in love
again and again every day

i don't really know myself
but i like who i am with you
i finally feel like a half-good person
after everything i've been through

and i only ever knew love to hurt and take
but you've taught me it gives and sustains
with the kind of blissful feeling
that makes me pinch myself in disbelief

but i don't ever want to wake up
i'd rather write shitty love poems
until the end of time
or for as long as i am so blessed
to call you mine

my home

there isn't a day that goes by
that i don't think about the left side
the route not taken

sometimes it calls me
whispers in my ears
wraps a blanket around my tired soul
and whispers 'come home.'

but then i remind myself
my home is not a cold building
with bars on windows and itchy blankets

my home is not
a busy street
where my mind can think
and my eyes can't see

my home is not
the midnight thoughts
and the pain racing through my body

i am not sure yet what my home is
but the rooms are slowly being constructed

as the walls get stronger
so too does my skin

it is decorated with everything i love

and i can't wait to move in.

www.ingramcontent.com/pod-product-compliance
Lightning Source LLC
Chambersburg PA
CBHW051753130826
49812CB00033B/1126
* 9 7 8 9 3 5 7 4 4 3 5 2 4 *